Christine was born in Liverpool, the youngest of three children. Her father died when she was eleven but her mother remarried an American, and the family emigrated when Christine was sixteen. After eight years, one of which was spent at the University of Berkeley, California, Christine returned to England, and two years later she married her childhood sweetheart. In 1995, the couple moved to the Irish Republic with their younger daughter, Tina, and settled in the rural west of the country.

I would like to dedicate this book to my husband, Tony, who took the journey with me but who, sadly, passed away on March 19, 2023.

Christine Baldock

OVER THE HILL

AUSTIN MACAULEY PUBLISHERS™

LONDON • CAMBRIDGE • NEW YORK • SHARJAH

A CIP catalogue record for this title is available from the British Library.

ISBN 9781035861637 (Paperback)
ISBN 9781035861644 (ePub e-book)

www.austinmacauley.com

First Published 2024
Austin Macauley Publishers Ltd®
1 Canada Square
Canary Wharf
London
E14 5AA

I would like to thank Nick Williamson of Peacehaven, who extracted a promise from me in 2016 to write this account of our move to Ireland. It has taken me seven years, but I try to keep my promises.

Chapter One

The Move to Ireland

This is a story of modern-day pioneering. No Conestoga wagons here, only an eight-year-old Ford Escort estate. But, just like those hardy souls who tracked westward across America's mighty rivers, deserts, and mountain ranges in their search for a better life in the 1800s, leaving behind everything that was familiar still meant taking that first step into the unknown—taking that leap of faith without a parachute.

And I must admit that it was my fault that we found ourselves living halfway up the side of a mountain in the wilds of East Clare in the Republic of Ireland.

At the age of fifty-three, my husband, Tony, expressed a desire to learn to ride a horse, so I arranged a riding lesson for him at our local riding school as a surprise. Little did I know what a Pandora's Box I was opening! Very soon, he was competing locally in jumping and cross country. And then, of course, he had to have his own horse and even took a second job to pay for it. It was a big twelve-year-old chestnut gelding called Basil Brush. Basil was sixteen and a half hands and had been used for hunting for the previous nine years.

This was the Maggie Thatcher era, and it was her opinion that everyone had the right to put themselves into debt for twenty-five years and own their own home. This, naturally, pushed up the interest rate. We were about two years into our mortgage, and when the rate reached double figures, it became evident that we couldn't afford the hay and straw, the hard feed, the renting of the field and the stable, the shoeing, and the vet's fees, as well as the mortgage. Something had to go, either the house or the horse. No prizes for guessing which one.

Our problem was that there wasn't enough equity in the house to purchase both enough land for Basil and a house for us, so we looked around for land that we could afford and that we could build on. England was not an option. "Planning Permission" was not in the vocabulary. At that time, many English people had exiled themselves to Brittany where property was cheap, but the country was full of foreigners who didn't speak English, and Tony was not prepared to learn another language. The Scottish Outer Hebrides were also considered; land was reasonably priced there. However, Tony considered Scotland too cold in winter.

Our friends, Stuart and Wendy, suggested that we join them for a holiday in the west of Ireland. This was 1993. They had discovered that one could buy a few acres, sometimes with a derelict cottage, for a fraction of the price of something comparable in the UK. They were also planning to move to Ireland, so we travelled across the Pond together in the hope of finding out how far our money would go. Starting in Cork and working our way up the west coast as far as Westport in Mayo, we looked at several parcels of land and got a feel for the country. Tony and I fell in love with Ireland.

In February of 1995, we had a buyer for our house, and we took another trip to Ireland. Our first choice for our new home was two and a half acres on the coast of Mayo with the hills behind and the sea in front. A lovely location, but on further investigation at the planning office, we discovered that there was no possibility of our getting planning. So, we continued south and settled on four and a half acres in East Clare, not far from the village of Flagmount and Lough Graney, and with a view of the Slievenoir Mountains.

The plot consisted of five fields on the side of a valley with a stream running through them. The stream joined up with another ditch flowing alongside the length of the access track as far as the country lane, where it passed under the road and continued through the far field and emptied into a fast-flowing river. The land itself was very poor, covered in sedge grass, nettles, and waist-high reeds, all of which attested to the wet ground. The access track was about a quarter of a mile long and very crude, with large blocks of stone brought down from the quarry and laid in the ruts. Ann and her partner, Frit, had five acres and a small stone cottage on the other side of the valley, and they had to reinforce the track to allow them to get their converted horsebox onto their land.

I knew that we would have to spend the next few years working hard to create a home. My mother, in Florida, had been recently widowed for the second time, and she was anxious for me to stay with her for a few weeks before we became too involved with our new life. So, Tony and Basil moved onto Wendy and Stuart's land while we completed the paperwork on the Irish property. Tina, our younger daughter, was in her summer holiday, so she and I took the opportunity of travelling to America to spend six weeks with my mother, leaving Tony to sort out our belongings and arrange for Basil's transportation to Ireland.

Whilst in the US, Mother and I dropped into a second-hand bookshop, and, as fate would have it, I found a book written by a retired schoolteacher living in New England who, with her husband, had practiced self-sufficiency all her life. Together, they had built several homes and outbuildings using field stones and concrete between wooden forms. Her description of the method and materials they used was detailed and almost pedantic, explaining exactly how they made the forms, assembled them, and bolted them together, in preparation for filling them with concrete and stones to make the walls. I thought, *I could do that!*

Eat your heart out, John Seymour!

So, on our return to England, Tina and I packed up the Escort Estate with some bare essentials and departed for Ireland, leaving Tony to continue sorting. We took with us two sleeping bags, my complete set of knitting needles, a manual sewing machine, two cats in their individual baskets, and Tina's hamster. What else would one need for pioneering? It wasn't exactly Desert Island Discs, but the theory was the same.

When we drove off the ferry onto the Irish roads, I thought there was a power cut. There were no street lights! But we headed west as the sun came up, stopping for breakfast along the way. I followed the directions the estate agent gave us and awarded myself twenty brownie points when we reached the track. I eased the car along it and parked at the head of the valley where the track turned towards Frit and Ann's cottage.

We took the two cat baskets out and carried them across the ditch, through the two fields towards a big Rowan tree that dominated the site.

The poor cats had been in their baskets for thirty-six hours at this point, so we had to take a chance and let them out. They hadn't eaten or drunk anything in all that time, nor had they made a mess in their cages. I left their food and water inside their baskets and set them free. I had to go off and find something for us to live in for a week or two until we could install a caravan, and hoped the cats would stay under the tree near their baskets. I was quite prepared for one or both of them to go feral.

We drove into Ennis for our shopping. I bought a two-man bell tent, a ditching spade, a little gas stove with some cans of gas, a kettle, and a couple of camping-size pans. When we arrived back at the land, one cat was waiting for us. The other was nowhere in sight. As the hours went by, I became convinced that we would never see him again. I was taking a late-night stroll with my flashlight when I felt a furry presence against my leg, and there he was. After all these years, I am still amazed that they didn't run off. That bell tent was our first home on the land, and we later immortalised it by creating a circular flower bed in the exact spot where we pitched our tent.

The tent wasn't ideal, but it gave us a breathing space while we looked around for a second-hand mobile home. Where we came from in Cornwall, second-hand caravans and mobile homes were very cheap. Holiday parks would replace their three-year-old vans with new ones, and the older vans would be auctioned off at a ridiculously low price. It didn't work that way here, but I took what I could. I bought a twenty-eight-foot caravan from Bunratty and arranged to have it delivered at the end of the week. While we waited excitedly for our new home to arrive, Tina and I filled the dry stream bed with rocks, which we had to carry in our arms from all over the property so that the caravan could cross. The bridge would come later. Although we had viewed the land in the pouring rain, with the streams and ditches rushing with water, now, perhaps luckily as it turned out, there wasn't a drop anywhere. All the streams had gone underground. Apparently, there hadn't been any measurable rain from April to September!

The caravan must have been delivered on a low loader because it had no A-frame for towing. (I imagine this was intentional on the part of the Bunratty firm so that customers would need their services to move the caravan at any time.) It suddenly appeared, deposited unceremoniously in the lane at the end of our access road, completely blocking the lane. Now, in the course of a day, we might see a couple of cars passing the end of our access. It's a country road and rarely used. But, as soon as the caravan was unloaded there, a queue of cars formed. I sent Tina to the next farm to ask for help in moving the van with his tractor, while I passed down the line of cars, apologising in my "terribly English" voice. "I'm so sorry to keep you waiting. I've sent for a tractor. I'm sure it won't be long." At that point, our neighbour, Niall, appeared, bouncing along on his little Massey Ferguson, waving a length of blue rope above his head like a lariat, and yelling, "There's no A-frame. She says there's no A-frame."

In response to my twittering, the last driver in the queue of cars said (and I quote), "Ye won't get that feckin' van down that feckin' track with that feckin' yoke." And he reversed smartly down the lane. Not being familiar with the vernacular, I was convinced that the driver must be terribly angry to use such language. It was not an auspicious start.

Niall threaded his rope underneath the caravan from one side to the other and began hauling it, oh so slowly, along our rough track. Unfortunately, because it wasn't fixed at each side but free to move, the van developed a distinct swing from side to side, and like a pendulum, the more it swayed, the more it was inclined to sway until it swayed itself into the ditch at the side of the track. Two hours and one trolley jack later, away we went again, inch by inch. Niall managed to drag the van, laboriously, a quarter of a mile to the place where Tina and I had filled the ditch with rocks. He turned it ready to cross the stream, and it settled comfortably into the bog. That's where it spent the night while I dreamed of it sinking slowly until it disappeared.

We had reinforcements the following day. The driver who had seemed so angry the day before (I learnt his name was Joe) turned up with his much bigger tractor. Joe studied the grounded caravan and said, "No problem." Between them, Niall and Joe managed to overcome the van's inertia, and it started to move. To my horror, this leviathan became wedged with its front end on our land, its rear end still in the bog, and its wheels spinning uselessly in mid-air above the empty stream bed. Joe's comment was, "Now, we have a problem."

With his trusty bowsaw to clear the branches complicating everything, a couple of trolley jacks, and two more recruits, Joe and Niall, with their tractors in tandem, hauled the van up the slope of the land, through the reeds and the rough grass, to its final resting place. A back panel was torn off the back of the caravan, Joe's radiator sprung a leak and boiled up, and

Niall's blue rope had simply disintegrated. But the van was in position.

Niall levelled it with rocks using a bowl full of water as a guide. Then he disappeared. and came back with a gas cylinder and attached, it for me. Before we could stop him, he dived under the van. "I'll just test for gas leaks," he said. Minutes later, he crawled out. "Everything is fine," he told me. "How did you test it?" I asked. I hadn't had time to reach for the Fairy Liquid. "I ran my lighter along the pipes," he told me. I think I would have been happier if I hadn't asked. But we had a home.

Chapter Two

Once the caravan was in situ, my next priorities were to get Tina enrolled in school as the autumn term had already started and to see about a job. Both tasks were a good bit more difficult than I had anticipated. The Principal of our chosen school in Gort was more concerned that Tina should have her full uniform than that she should have her textbooks and stationery, and refused to allow her in the school without her uniform. I imagine he had frequently accommodated the children of some of the influx of English Travellers, only to have them leave after a few weeks, so he required an investment in the uniform to ensure they stayed. Unfortunately, I only had the funds to provide Tina either with her books or the uniform, not both. By the time she was fully kitted out, the books were no longer available. We managed to get some second-hand books, and for the remainder of the time, she had to make do with sharing with a classmate. I'm afraid that the initial interview with the Principal was the beginning of a four-year battle with the education system. Although, I must admit that some of Tina's problems were of her own making.

The jobs front was just as depressing. There simply weren't any. I couldn't get dole money, and until my husband joined me, I wasn't entitled to child allowance. I was told that we were my husband's responsibility and that he should send money over to me. I passed that message on to Tony, and he promised to forward what he could. Of course, the post would take three working days, and there was no movement of post on the weekend. So, it was then a Wednesday, and I wouldn't have access to any money until the following Monday. After spending out on Tina's uniform, I had exactly two pence left, no food, and very little petrol in the car. And then… Sod's law… I had a couple of visitors.

Frit and his partner, Ann, had arrived in the valley three months before us. They had ferried slabs of stone from the quarry above us to lay on the track and enable them to get their converted horsebox onto their five acres on the far side of the bog. They had been New Age Travellers for several years and had bought the land simply because they were tired of being moved on. Ann was from Scotland, blonde, articulate, and well-educated. She was wearing faded denim dungarees with one top clip missing so that the bib was flapping loosely. She was wearing boots with the laces untied and tucked into the tops. Wisps of hair drifted across her face, and she frequently tossed her head or brushed them aside in what might have been a nervous gesture.

The first thing one noticed about Frit was how hirsute he was. He had thick dusty dreadlocks that hung past his elbows, a thick beard, and an enormous moustache. In amongst all this hair was a round baby face, twinkling blue eyes, and a cheeky grin. When he spoke, it was with a Birmingham dialect. He, too, wore bovver boots with the laces undone. His trousers were tucked into the tops of his boots, and he appeared to be wearing several layers of shirts under an army greatcoat that reached nearly to his ankles. I apologised for not offering them a cup of tea and cake, and I joked about coming up empty-handed after shaking every money tree I could think of. We chatted for a while, and then they left.

I took a bowl and began picking blackberries, which were growing in abundance all over the property. How on earth would Tina and I survive until money arrived from Tony on Monday'? I had no idea where to go for help in this strange country.

(Months later, I was reprimanded by John and Annette, who kept the general store in the village of Flagmount, for not going to them for help when we first arrived, but, of course, I didn't know that at the time. I learnt later that many of us in the area could not have managed without the generosity of John and Annette and their family.)

Totally absorbed with my worries, I didn't see Frit arrive until I heard his unmistakeable voice. He had walked back. He handed me forty punts, rubbed his nose in embarrassment, and said, "I imagine you could use this." He made some remark about preferring something more substantial than blackberries for tea and went away. I shall never forget his kindness that day. He didn't know me, and he couldn't be certain that he'd get his money back, but had he not loaned me that forty punts, Tina and I would have been in desperate straits by Monday.

As soon as he had gone, we jumped in the car, limped down to the shop, free-wheeled the last few yards to the petrol pumps, put the petrol in, bought a few groceries, and filled up the container for drinking water. We were as rich as Croesus! When we arrived home, we began the arduous task of transporting the food and water across the stream bed, the walls, and the fields. I was determined to begin creating a driveway from the track to the caravan.

The following day, I made a start, measuring out an eight-foot-wide stretch for the one hundred yards or so from the stream to our door. Of course, as yet, there was no bridge, but that would come later. I skimmed off the turf with my trusty ditching spade and piled it up beside the trench. I planned to dig out about six inches, then put down hardcore and finish off with gravel. After two days of hard graft (remember, this was a virgin field of sedge grass and reeds), I had managed to dig out quite a length, and then the weather broke, and the rains came, so I scuttled for shelter in the caravan. The following day, there was an eight-foot-wide river where I had dug my "driveway." Clearly, I needed some advice.

Dermott, the neighbour who, along with his brother Joe, had helped to manhandle the caravan into position, brought his tractor and finger bar. He cut a swathe through the reeds so that we could bring our shopping across the fields without getting soaked to the waist. While we were having a cup of tea afterwards, I told him about my attempt at a driveway. He told me, "In Ireland we don't dig down. We start at ground level and build up." I knew Dermott was familiar with the land because he had grown up in the area and had allowed his cattle to roam at will on the side of the valley. His cattle would start at the road and graze across Frit's side of the valley, along the ridge at the top end, and then through the stream onto our few acres. The land had been "commonage" for nine of the local farmers until the English came and began fencing it off.

I had plans to eventually sink a well, and I am a great believer in consulting the local people for advice and information, so I said, "Dermott, you know this land. Where do you think would be a good place to dig a well?" He answered succinctly, "Where the feckin' water is."

Tina's birthday was on the 29th September, and we still had very little money.

The only "gift" I could give her was a day off school, and she spent the whole day playing in the stream. We had a small iced cake with one candle, and we cooked our meal in the middle of the table on the primus stove. She asked for two laying hens for her birthday, and I promised she would have them when her dad was there to make the hen coop. We were both looking forward to his arrival because there was so much that needed to be done before the winter.

The day came. A Cornish friend had arranged transport for the horse, Basil, and Tony's pride and joy was unloaded at the next farm into one of their stables because we had no fences as yet. Our friend followed the horsebox in his van with all our goods that Tony deemed essential for our new life, and he continued on while Basil was being settled and the stockmen were given refreshment. It was pouring with rain, wind-driven horizontally, and the darkness had descended early. Frit and Ann appeared from nowhere in their wet weather gear to see if they could help.

Tony and I had agreed to get rid of everything except those items that would be of use to us because we had no storage facilities. Of course, we also had no electricity, no sewerage or running water. What we desperately needed was a wheelbarrow, gardening tools, anything petrol-driven like a chainsaw and a brush-cutter, a mattock and pick to attack the clumps of grass and reeds, and a wrecking bar to lever the rocks out of the ground, and things like a hammer, a level, and builders line, nails, and screws, the list went on and on.

The first thing that came out of the furniture van and into the lashing rain was… a television. Tony struggled to carry it across the raging stream, two wet slippery walls, and two muddy fields to reach the caravan.

Tina and I were laughing so hard, much to his annoyance, that we couldn't even help him!

It was far too arduous to get the contents of the furniture van to the caravan that night, so Frit suggested that we create a "tack pile" just inside the bottom field with a tarpaulin on the ground and spread the goods on that.

Then we could cover them with another tarpaulin and address the problem over the next few days. That "tack pile" remained there for ten months! It included some electrical goods which were useless and several books which were ruined except for one particular volume. It was the Bible, the only book that survived the ten months under the tarpaulin in the wind and weather.

Chapter Three

We chose to move to Ireland to live amongst Irish people, only to find ourselves surrounded by English. I believe it was towards the end of the influx of New Age Travellers who wanted to live "off the grid." Because we lived in a caravan, we were labelled as "hippies" or worse. And we occasionally came across anti-English sentiments. (Several caches of arms were discovered in the first few months we were here.)

One day, Tina came home from school in tears. The History class had been studying the Great Potato Famine of 1841–49, and she had been made to feel responsible. At the next PTA meeting, we met the History teacher, a lovely man, who told us that he had felt so sorry for Tina that he had decided to switch to a different subject—the American War of Independence. Then, he had suddenly realised "Oh no! The Redcoats!" We have also been considered to blame for what Henry VIII did to the monasteries and for what Oliver Cromwell did to the churches and abbeys. Mind you, they didn't do much for the monasteries, churches, and abbeys in the UK, either. And don't even mention the Black and Tans!

The other problem Tina had was that she was not Catholic. In English schools, there was a non-sectarian service each morning at assembly. Any Religious Instruction is also non-sectarian. Furthermore, the children are given an understanding of other world religions. In Ireland, R.I. is solely on Catholicism and the Catechism. I contacted the school and persuaded the teacher to allow Tina to sit at the back of the class and do her homework. First, though, I had to convince her that Tina had received a moral upbringing, albeit under the influence of the Church of England. Tina was also exempted from having to learn the Irish language. The teacher considered that, as Tina was thirteen when she arrived, she only had two years before she was due to take the Junior Certificate, and it was unrealistic to expect her to catch up. She took Spanish instead and did very well.

It was a blessing that Tina was allowed to spend some of her day doing homework. With no electricity, we had to rely on gas lights and candles. The poor child often had to do her homework by candlelight. I remember on one occasion that she had to provide herself with a clean apron for a Domestic Science examination, and, although her apron was pristine clean, I had no iron. The teacher embarrassed her in front of the class by making her use the school laundry facilities. By and large, the teaching staff at the Gort secondary school were very good to Tina, especially Sister de Lourdes, who gave her extra tuition in Mathematics and helped her to pass her exams.

We had replaced the gas fire with a wood-burning stove, cleverly made from an empty gas container. I was constantly buying candles, all types, all colours. I saved the stubby ends to use as firelighters in the stove. Then I decided to make my own dipped candles. I bought the wick and some clear wax, but I also added some stubby ends to the mix along with some wax crayons for colour. Whatever I could recycle was melted down in a clean baked beans tin. And, of course, the mix of red, blue, and green got darker and darker until the candles I was turning out were almost black. It came back to me via the village grapevine that Tony and I were holding Black Masses with our black candles!

One thing I learnt from those early days was that if you had food, fuel, clothing, and shelter, everything else was a luxury.

There was a sub-culture of English and Irish Travellers at that time. Nobody had any money, and there was little hope of employment, although there was plenty of talent and expertise among the community. So, they devised their own currency based on "Letts," which operated exactly like real money with a "banker" to keep a record of the transactions. There was even a "Letto" held each month. Anyone with any skill or talent could advertise it and be paid in Letts. It seemed to have worked quite well in the short term. We arrived at the tail end of it and never got involved. It seemed that, as the system began to collapse, everyone wanted to be paid in punts instead, and some devotees of the system found themselves with hundreds of Letts and nowhere to spend them.

That first October, after Tony joined us, we were invited to a Letts sale which was held in the GAA Hall in Scariff. All the goods on sale were hand-made. The majority of both the vendors and the customers seemed to be "hippies." Headbands and Jesus sandals, with beads and wool braided into the hair, was the uniform. It was straight out of the sixties, although I felt we did it better first time around when the battle cry was "Make love, not war." They were selling alternative medicines and lotions made from aloe vera and comfrey, beautifully decorated "dream catchers," knitted items, and pottery. There were home-baked cakes, home-grown fruit and vegetables, and even a couple of puppies for sale.

There was an Alsatian bitch advertised for sale on a flyer inside the hall, and outside there were two puppies of dubious parentage with their mother. The mother was a brown Labrador, and the puppies' father was a Newfoundland, but there was Collie in there somewhere as well. The pups were visiting everyone in the yard. The male came to me, but his sister pushed him out of the way to get my attention. He accepted it good-naturedly and moved on to someone else. Of course, the female then lost interest. Now, my ideal dog has always been an Alsatian, and we certainly needed a dog, isolated as we were.

Tina said that if I would choose one, she would get it for me for Christmas. The owner of the Alsatian wanted quite a bit of money for it, far more than Tina could afford. I looked at the two brown puppies and Tina's eager face. She could get the puppy for free, only paying the price of a dog license. "I'd like the boy," I told her, and she scampered off to negotiate for the dog. Our neighbour, Kate, took the female puppy to keep her white Alsatian company and agreed to hang onto Tina's puppy until Christmas. Tina would collect him on Christmas morning.

The Employment Office recognised that it was unlikely that Tony would find employment at his age, so they moved him from the unemployment list and put him onto Early Retirement. The money was the same, but it was a way of reducing the unemployment figures. We both did odd jobs, whatever we could find as long as it was legal. We frequently did gardening and were often paid in meat. I designed and knitted sweaters which I sold in a craft cooperative in Scariff.

Wendy and I worked in a hotel on Saturday nights, and I also had babysitting duties. Tony, with his farming background, could look after Kate's horses when required. He even assisted Joe and Dermott when one of their young cows was having difficulties delivering a big bull calf. He enjoyed working with wood and would make pig pens and fox-proof poultry sheds for a lady called Annie O'Donnell (no direct relation to Joe and Dermott).

When I was in Ireland on my own, before Tony joined me, Annie walked over the hill and through the fields to shake me by the hand and welcome me to Ireland. I thought that was a lovely gesture. Indeed, she was a lovely woman. She would use local talent for her odd jobs, regardless of nationality or religion. She was totally non-judgemental. She always fed her workers well and overpaid them too. During the first summer, we were conscripted to help Annie foot her turf on the bog, a hot and back-breaking job, and something Tony and I had never come across before. Weeks later, we were again conscripted to help load up the turf. On that autumn day, it was windy, raining, cold, and miserable. Tony and I managed to collect up the turf until about eight in the evening, and then Annie took us around to her place and made us a hot toddy. She made the best hot whisky and lemon this side of the pond. I believe that hot toddy stopped us from getting pneumonia. Tony and I went home feeling pleased with ourselves and what we had accomplished, only to learn the following day that Annie had gone back to the bog and worked on until midnight!

Often, she would ring us up and ask, "What are ye at?" and if Tony would say that there was nothing at home needing his attention at that moment, she would say, "Can ye give me five minutes to put up some fencing?" We knew then that it would be a full day's job because her favourite saying was "While ye're here," but she was a good friend, and we never refused her whether it was a knitting job for me or a carpentry job for Tony. And whatever time of day it was, there was always a meal on the table and the hot whisky and lemon.

As Christmas approached that first year, we noticed some activity in the forestry on the other side of the lane. A car and trailer would travel up the road unloaded. The same car and trailer would travel back a few minutes later loaded with Christmas trees and with a Garda car in hot pursuit. Then the same car and trailer would come back the other way with its Garda escort, but it seemed that the Gardai had no intention of catching the tree thieves. It was like watching an episode of The Keystone Cops.

Our first Christmas was a very home-made affair with paper decorations, and our small tree was one which we dug up from the side of the road where it had self-sown, meaning to replant it once Christmas was over. I had made knitted presents for the family, and we went into debt for a turkey with all the trimmings. My present from Tina came bouncing up the field with a red bow around his neck and licked everyone within licking distance. Tina and Buster, the puppy, spent the remainder of Christmas Day using a black bag as a sledge and sliding down the field in the snow. We now had two hens producing eggs, a horse, and a dog. Our "wealth" was increasing.

***

I imagine that the New Age Travellers in our area had a problem deciding where on the social echelons we belonged. We were English. We lived in a caravan. We were obviously jobless and therefore impecunious. They invited us to all their raves until they realised that we were not accepting. They offered us something called "squidgy black" and passed around strange herbal cigarettes, which we always refused.

On one occasion, I was dog sitting for Frit (of the dreadlocks), and the dog led me along a well-trodden path, which was clearly familiar to her. It passed through waist-high weeds and scrub and ended up at a patch of well-cultivated soil about four metres square, containing some very healthy plants that bore a resemblance to tomatoes. Another of our neighbours grew his illicit crop in a clearing in the forestry, and yet another had a four-foot section at the end of his cottage fitted with ultraviolet lamps where he grew his plants, and we understood that you could only access this "garden" through a secret door behind the fireplace.

Apart from these recreational drugs, including a small type of mushroom that grew in profusion all over our land, and which some of the travellers kindly offered to clear, the other currency at that time was homemade wine and poteen. When Frit's daughter was born, he turned up at our door with a bottle of poteen to wet the baby's head. I kept the men supplied with coffee, and Frit added poteen to the mugs. Before we had drunk the coffee, it was topped up with more poteen so eventually, we had no idea how much poteen we were drinking. I noticed that Tony was sliding down the back of his seat, and Frit was sliding down with him to carry on their conversation. It was evident that Frit was used to the local brew because Tony ended up, literally, under the table.

Frit offered to help me get him to bed, but I just covered my unconscious husband with a blanket. Then I watched Frit get into his car and drive up to his wagon on the other side of the valley, as straight and as sober as the proverbial judge. Tony, on the other hand, was hungover for three days and vowed never to touch poteen again.

This was the Ireland we came to in 1995.

Chapter Four

The Vegetable Garden

I started a small vegetable plot in a secluded part of the property before Tony joined us, but after we had talked it over, it was obvious that my little garden would be insufficient for our needs. We planted it with raspberry canes, blackcurrants, jostaberries (a cross between blackcurrants and gooseberries), and we created a raised strawberry bed. My little plot became the "fruit garden." We never managed to harvest any fruit from it because the birds always seemed to get there first!

We wanted to be as self-sufficient as possible, so it was decided that we would create a half-acre of vegetable plot in the field below the caravan. Tony wanted ten beds in two rows of five, each one twenty-four feet long and eight feet wide with walkways in between so that they could be worked from either side. The first row of five would be for potatoes because we knew that, with eggs and potatoes, at least we would not starve. The rest of the beds would be put to roots, brassicas, peas, and beans.

All the good gardening books tell you, "First, double dig your plot." But those gurus hadn't been presented with a virgin field that had never been cultivated. It had once been cut for hay, but even that was only suitable for bedding.

Furthermore, wherever and whenever I thrust my spade into the ground, I would be rewarded by the "clunk" of metal on stone. I soon learned to distinguish the difference in sound between a simple stone, a more serious rock, or a solid plate of mountain. We marked out the first of our plots and skimmed off the reeds and sedge grass, sometimes having to employ a mattock to remove the roots. Each neat square of turf was laid along the length of the bed in the hope that it would rot down and could be added back as humus. We discovered that we had about three inches of topsoil, underneath which was about ten inches of grey clay from which we probably could have manufactured pots. Beneath that, there was mountain, causing us to encounter rocks with each spade thrust. We managed to lift some of the rocks out.

Some of them Tony broke up with a sledgehammer into manageable pieces, which were then removed. Larger boulders would take us all day to get out of the ground, using forestry poles to raise them enough to place rocks under for support. We repeated the process until the offending boulder was at ground level and could be hauled out. On a couple of occasions, we used the car to drag the boulder up a log ramp. Once smashed into smaller pieces, most of the rocks were spread on the infant driveway. If they refused to break up, they were dragged to a corner of the field as a "feature" as part of a rock garden. There was one enormous plate of rock that stretched from the vegetable plot across the driveway, and it simply had to stay there.

It took three weeks of hard labour to create each potato bed. With so much having been removed from them, they were well below the level of the rest of the land, and we had no compost nor well-rotted manure. So, we dug three trenches in each of our five beds right down to the rock, spread raw, fresh horse manure in each trench, and laid our seed potatoes on top. Then, we covered them up as best we could with whatever we could find. Strangely enough, we had the best crop of potatoes that year than any year after, and they came up ready washed from the rainwater flowing over the rock underneath them. By the end of May, we had ten beds up and running, with hopes of another ten the following year.

We sold some of our produce at the end of the Bog Road to cover the cost of our seed, leaving an "honesty box" on the vegetable stand. The locals called it The Corner Shop. We found that the honest box worked well. There were some days when I would find an IOU written on a scruffy bit of paper, but the money was always there the following day and frequently overpaid. We clamped the potatoes, made wine, and experimented with various ways of preserving. (Layering beans in salt doesn't work. It just produces salty, mushy beans.) I made a conserve out of Rowan berries, thinking it would make a tasty jam. That was a disaster! As jam, it tasted awful, so we thought it might make an accompaniment for meat. It still tasted awful. I had ten jars of disgusting, sticky Rowan jelly that I couldn't even give away. I stored it for four years and then gave it a decent burial in the corner of a field. But, over the years, we did accumulate about eight or ten demijohns of various wines, fruit, and vegetable, bubbling away in the tack room.

In those days, there was very little choice of fruit and vegetables in the shops. It was before the Celtic Tiger and before the influx of Brazilians, Nigerians, and Eastern

Europeans who introduced Ireland to their own ethnic foods. The only vegetables our Irish friends seemed to eat were carrots, onions, cabbage, and swede. One passerby bought a bunch of radishes from our "Corner Shop" at the end of the track, and a week later she met us and asked how she should cook these radishes. We explained that they were eaten raw in a salad, and I asked her why she had bought them if she didn't recognise them. She replied, "They looked pretty." We took some runner beans to Annie O'Donnell and watched as she snapped them in half and added them to the boiling water without trimming them or slicing them.

Just before our second Christmas, we asked the manager of the Gort Supervalu store if he could get some pomegranates, which Tony and I traditionally bought at that time of the year as well as pineapple, coconuts, and chestnuts. He managed to get one box, but ended up throwing most of them away. It seemed Tony and I were the only customers who bought them.

Looking at the array of exotic fruits and vegetables available now, it seems strange that the most exotic fruits in those days were oranges, bananas, and the occasional pineapple. Foreign travel and the influx of tourists have educated us to expect a greater and more exciting variety.

That second year, we also acquired more stock. A dog belonging to one of the travellers came onto our land and killed one of Tina's hens. The two of them, Brandy and Chocolate, had been great characters, strutting around together like two old maids, scrapping around for worms while we were digging, even getting their heads between the tines of Tony's fork to get at the prize. All they needed was a shoulder bag each and a poke bonnet. So, we were quite shocked to lose them so violently.

Our neighbour, Kate, wanted to reduce some of her stock of poultry to concentrate on raising pigs, and she kindly offered us six Light Sussex hens with a cockerel to keep them in order. She also promised Tina one of her lambs. I certainly had no objection because the lamb would be part Texel, which is renowned for its fleece. I harboured dreams of dyeing, spinning, and knitting up my own wool. Kate also kept milking goats, and in the springtime, when the day came for us to collect Tina's lamb, Kate had just pronounced the death sentence on a nanny kid superfluous to requirements. It was a cute little thing, the same age as the lamb, and it was about to be hit on the head with a sledgehammer. Of course, we couldn't allow that! So, we ended up taking both Narla the sheep and Snowdrop the goat, home in the back of the Escort Estate.

It was 1997, and the horses, both ours and Wendy's for a while, had been kept in their field by stringing baler twine between the posts and tying plastic strips from carrier bags onto it, which deterred them from trying to escape.

That string kept them in for a year. We had been buying fence posts at the rate of five a week and had borrowed a poster to get them in the ground. The poster is a metal tube with a handle on either side for lifting it over the post. With one of us on either side, we hammered the post into the ground. We aimed to position the posts at six-foot intervals, but there was always the problem of rocks in the very spot where we wanted the post. Also, we had a problem because of the disparity between my height and Tony's, and, of course, between my strength and his. He practically had to lift me as well as the poster! We made life more difficult for ourselves by positioning me on the downhill side of the task. We soon swapped sides. Over a period of time, we had both sides of the driveway fenced off with "slobs" (the first slice of bark from the logs, which has very little value to the owner of the woodyard.) It made an attractive rustic fence.

It was time to extend the vegetable plot. We asked Frit to turn over the ground for the next ten beds, thinking that they might be easier to dig. But before we could progress with the digging, disaster struck.

We had borrowed a car trailer to take some recyclable rubbish to the tip, which, at that time, was near Whitegate, off a narrow switchback of a lane and halfway up a hill. Tony saw a car approaching at great speed over the rise, and he pulled over as far as he could onto the verge, thinking that the other car would pull into the yard or at least slow down to ease past us. We assumed that since we had seen him, then he surely should have seen us.

Tony said, "He's not going to stop!" The other car appeared from over the rise, daylight showing under his wheels, as he bounced over the rise and landed on our bonnet. Hearing the crash, two lads came out of the recycling centre to see if we needed help. One of them remarked that the young driver must have been going at some speed.

Anyway, I took his details, refused his offer to "fix" our car himself, and we proceeded gingerly into the centre to unload our rubbish. We limped home with a crumpled bonnet. The car sustained three thousand punts damage. It was a write-off. Tony was suffering considerable back pain. We put in a claim to our insurance and heard nothing. Eventually, I contacted them, only to be told that we should have hired a solicitor to fight our case. Tony had several trips to Dublin to assess the injury to his back, and finally, after four years, he received compensation. But the accident changed everything. There was a lot of work he could no longer do, and it was clear that heavy digging was one of them. Ten plots were enough for me to manage and the second ten for which Frit cleared the ground were never completed.

Chapter Five

Problems Encountered

Back in 1995, the year we came to Ireland, I was alternately amused and irritated by the attitude of the menfolk and the way they treated women. I realise that there was probably a vast difference between the attitudes of the menfolk in the farming communities to those living in the towns, but it still exists today to a certain extent, especially in my age group. One lady told me that when she was a young girl she didn't expect to marry for love. They viewed marriage as a job. They contracted to look after a house, and provide their husband with children, make soda bread daily (failure to do so was grounds for annulment), help with the cattle and be responsible for the poultry. In return, their husband would provide for them. When electrification was introduced in rural Ireland, every household along the line had to agree to the installation. Some farmers were against it because they believed it would make their wives lazy! I asked one farmer's wife at what age women retired in Ireland. Her response was, "When they die."

The farmhouses we visited were quite spartan, often with a tiled or even flagstone floor. There were very few soft furnishings such as carpets or rugs on the floor, no cushions on the chairs, no ornaments or plants. All these feminine touches were absent possibly because the men controlled the expenditure of money. But Irish hospitality and welcome were always there. No matter what time of day it was, out would come the soda bread, the butter, and the jam, and with a big pot of tea poured from a kettle off the iron stove. Frequently, we were encouraged to have a plate of cold meat and a salad with the bread and butter.

One of our neighbours, a lovely man called Jimmy Fahy who, alas, is no longer with us, had given Tony a bale of hay for our horses, delivering it to us with his tractor. He wouldn't take any money for it, so we decided to take him a can of diesel. He invited us in, and he was clearly delighted with the visit. He proudly showed us his cattle shed where every animal had its own compartment—no slatted shed for him—and he touched each of them on the rump as he walked down the aisle. The shed was immaculate. There was no smell of urine or manure. One could tell how fond he was of his cattle.

Inside his farmhouse, the living room was spotless with a flagstone floor so clean one could have eaten off it. The only furniture was a table with two wooden chairs. He moved the chairs to either side of the wide fireplace and told us to sit in front of the open log fire. Then, he disappeared into the kitchen. He reappeared a few moments later and gave Tony a glass of whisky, while we waited for the tea. To my amusement, he handed me a glass of water. Perhaps, in Jimmy's world, a woman didn't expect to drink spirits with the menfolk. But when the teapot arrived, I was invited to pour the tea for all of us. Dear Jimmy never had a bad word to say about anyone and always thought the best of people.

Seamus, Annie's husband, was a prime example of the attitudes of the time towards women. All their children were grown up, but they still called him "Boss." He had his own chair at the head of the table, and when he caught Annie sitting in his chair, I saw him oust her with a gesture of his thumb and a toss of his head. He could also put his booted feet on the table, but woe betide anyone else who tried it. But Seamus was a great character with a fantastic memory for songs and stories and the history of the area. The only difficulty we had was that when he narrated events, he would assume that we knew the people of whom he spoke, as though we had grown up with them as he had. On one occasion, Tony asked Seamus about a cottage he had noted along a nearby lane, and Seamus said, "I've told you this before. Now, I'll tell you again, and pay attention this time." He should have been a schoolmaster!

A few months after we had started building, Seamus asked me, "Christina, how did you learn your trade?"

I told him, "You'll laugh when I tell you, Seamus." He replied, "Try me."

"Well," I told him, "I read a book."

His response was immediate. "JESUS MARY MOTHER O' GOD!"

Tony and I were digging out the foundations for the first half of the house when Seamus turned up in the company of a man we didn't know. He was introduced to us as Mr Halnon, who was a builder. He had worked in stone and had heard of my ambition to build a stone house, and he wanted to inspect my work. It would have been rude of me to refuse, so I told Seamus to go ahead. They strolled all around the stable block, and the visitor touched some of the stones, deep in discussion with Seamus. They stood back and studied the walls, pointing and touching and talking. Then, the visitor came over to where I was standing deep in the footings.

"I see you've done the rear wall in stone as well, and crossed all your joins." He paused. "There's only one thing wrong with it," he said.

I was quite prepared for criticism, and I was always anxious to improve on what I had done, but my heart sank. I was terrified that I would have to employ a bulldozer to pull the lot down.

"What's that, Mr Halnon?" I asked.

"Well," he repeated, "There's only one thing wrong with it. A woman built it!" And he stamped off down the driveway.

I used to have difficulty getting the builders' merchants to take me seriously. I was ordering some concrete lintels, and I gave the lad who served me the dimensions I wanted. He insisted on talking to Tony and ignoring me. So, Tony finally pointed to me and said, "Don't ask me, ask the builder." Then, he wanted to know the size of the "hole" and explained at great length that the lintels should extend beyond the span of the window by several inches either side. I'm quite certain he wouldn't have treated a male customer in that way. If I went into a builders' provider in Gort, I would stand waiting to be served as though I were invisible, while the tradesmen would receive attention ahead of me, and I would eventually have to approach the counter and jump up and down to be served.

However, a lovely man called Joe Spain, who owned the woodyard with which we dealt, was one of the few men who listened to me with respect. He had a love of all kinds of wood, and I had set my heart on having oak trim above my windows and doors. He and I would sit side by side on a log, roll ourselves a cigarette each, and discuss what I needed. Each of my windows and doors in my two-foot-thick walls has two concrete lintels to support the weight of the wall above, and an oak lintel both inside and out as a trim to set off the stonework.

I think the best compliment we had was when the building was almost finished, and one friend told us that, at the beginning, the whole village was laughing at us. "But they are not laughing now," he said.

Chapter Six

The valley in between our property and Frit's was called "Carheen" by the locals, which apparently means "a slough" or "a low-lying place" in Irish. In other words, a bog. If we stood on the edge of it while a hefty vehicle like a large tractor or a lorry passed along the access road, we could feel the ground moving in ripples like the old-time cakewalk at the fairground. It was covered in reeds, bog myrtle, and coarse grasses that could also dry out in warm weather. The hills around us were planted with fir trees and the occasional patch of larch. Some of the plantings were privately owned, but most belonged to Coilte, the government forestry department.

Every year, as the weather warmed up, there was always the danger of fire that could decimate the forestry plantations, started sometimes with malice or just carelessness. Sometimes a broken piece of glass can magnify the sun's rays and start a fire. Sometimes, a cigarette thrown thoughtlessly from a passing car onto the dry sedge grass will catch light. Sometimes, a petrol-soaked rag and a match can deliberately ruin acres of timber. More often than not, it was a matter of youngsters looking for some excitement.

One year, while we were still living in the caravan, there were three fires set in our area, and the Gardai eventually caught the teenagers who were responsible.

That day, Tony noticed that there were flames on the bog near the road. By the time we had run to our gateway, a matter of about a hundred metres, the wind had got behind the fire, and it was approaching with the speed of a train. It was a monstrous, frightening beast, trailing black smoke and consuming everything in its path. It was a huge tube about five metres in diameter of purple, red, orange, and yellow, spanning the valley from one side to the other, and curling back on itself as though attempting to sting itself in the tail. As it roared past our gateway, the noise of it was like the sound of an angry mob.

The heat it generated singed the hairs on our arms, and the air was so polluted by the smoke that each breath we took burned in our throats.

Within seconds, the monster had reached the end of the valley where the access road turned towards the far hills. For a few moments, it seemed to consider its options, frustrated by finding its progress impeded by the track, and died down a little, sullen and glowering. Now was our chance to get ahead of it. It would either skip across the track and continue up the end of the valley towards a derelict property. Or it could turn toward the far hill and threaten the cottage that Frit and Ann were renovating. Beyond that was the forestry and the smallholding belonging to Kate and Nyall. But its appetite wasn't satisfied yet. It flared again, changed direction, and headed for the clump of trees that concealed Frit's little cottage.

With scarves over our faces, we raced through the smoke to reach the cottage, determined that the beast wouldn't claim it. By this time, our ranks had swelled to about twenty, and we made our stand in front of the building. Armed with anything that could hold water, we damped down the vegetation ahead of the fire. We could hear it spitting and snarling beyond the grove of trees.

Then—the sound we dreaded! In one, hissing gulp, the monster devoured a tree, stripping it of pine needles and leaving only the charred branches. Again and again, its fiery tongue flashed upwards, denuding each tree as it "crowned." Each one accompanied with a loud WHOOSH. By now, it was only feet away.

Then, it suddenly halted. Perhaps we defeated it with our wet earth strategy. Perhaps it simply got tired of the game, but the beast was now contained.

Jubilant, we congratulated each other, rejoicing in our teamwork, our neighbourliness, and our sense of community. We shook each other by the hand, introducing ourselves. Beer cans and mugs of tea appeared with biscuits and cake. No one had been injured. No property had been damaged. And so, we celebrated.

But I don't suppose any one of us gave a thought to the lone marsh tit wheeling and diving in the acrid sky, keening and calling, searching for her nest of youngsters in the blackened bog.

***

One of the worst things about the early days on the hillside was the midges. They arrived in April and were with us until

October. As soon as the sun came up, they descended on the caravan like heat-seeking missiles, and in the beginning, they surrounded the caravan to a depth of at least a metre. Just leaving the caravan meant having to run the gauntlet. Darkness didn't deter them. Rain didn't get rid of them. The only thing that discouraged them was limestone or excessive heat to "burn" them off. So, we could either stay inside until the sun was sufficiently hot, which was rarely, or leave home early in the morning and head for the Burren, which is an area of limestone—and no midges.

At first, we tried working through them, even covering our heads with veils made of net curtains. We tried several sprays and creams. (The most effective was a body lotion by Avon!) Being so tiny, they could get through the smallest crack. Inside the caravan, while we read or played board games in the evening, the midges would fly up to the gas lights above the table in a kamikaze action. Killed by the heat, they would float down onto the surface of the table. By the end of the evening, there would be a pile of the tiny insects under the light. *(Enough to make a sandwich, Tony said.)* They even managed to get inside our bed. I had to get up one morning at five o'clock because I was being stung. I took Buster and walked up the hill in the cool of the morning to get some relief. As long as I kept moving, I stayed midge-free.

But as soon as I stopped to take in the view, these heat-seeking missiles zoned in on me.

Of course, the animals suffered from the midges too. They would also keep on the move, sometimes all night long, to try to escape them and be exhausted the following day. We have seen our white Saanen goat, Snowdrop, absolutely black with them. We had to wipe the horses' faces with a cloth soaked in repellent because the tiny pests go for the moisture in the eyes.

There seemed to be optimum temperatures for the presence of the midges. In the early morning, there would be a cloud of them surrounding the caravan. If it turned hot, they would disappear and then return when the temperature dropped. Happily, as we progressed with the building of the house, the problem began to ease. I imagine it was the lime in the cement that discouraged them. However, we have also seen a reduction in the number of swallows that used to build their nests in the stables and the eaves. I have heard that a single swallow can consume three thousand midges in a day. I wonder who counted them!

On 31st October, we came home to find literally millions of swallows wheeling over the bog from one end to the other in a constant oval flight path extending about half a mile long from the road to the head of the valley and about thirty feet high. It went on and on. We assumed that they were picking up insects as they skimmed over the reeds and grasses, and then up into the air again and back towards the road. The noise of their beating wings and their twittering was almost deafening. It seemed amazing to us that, with the sheer number of them, it was miraculous that they didn't collide.

The following day, there was absolute silence in the valley, and not a single swallow was seen anywhere in the area. We could only assume that they had gathered for a last orgy of eating before commencing their incredible journey to the south of Africa. We have never seen another display like it, nor such a huge assembly of swallows in one place.

Chapter Seven

Our Pets and Other Animals

As I mentioned in Chapter Three, the first pet we acquired was Buster, a fantastic dog that Tina gave me for Christmas that first year. He was not a particularly attractive dog. There was Border Collie and Labrador in his family tree, but the breed that defined him was that of his grandmother, a Newfoundland. She had to be shot for sheep worrying. And Buster's great uncle, also a Newfoundland, of course, who had to be kept chained up all his life. Buster was big, and he had the webbed feet of a Newfie. When he was fully grown, there was no point telling him that there was nothing left on the table because he was able to check for himself!

When Buster was only a few months old, we visited Niall and Kate, who had a white Alsatian. Their dog immediately attacked our pup, hurting his leg and making him yelp. Months later, the white Alsatian visited us. Buster, now fully grown, threw him on his back and stood over him, smiling a wide smile just inches from the dog's throat. That was the only time I can remember him being aggressive towards anything, animal, or human. However, there were two men he didn't like: one, because he always arrived on a noisy Harley Davidson, and the other simply because he was loud and boisterous. If either of these gentlemen arrived at our gate, he would be met by a very big dog who would lead him up to our door by the wrist, held gently but firmly in the dog's mouth. If the visitor tried to pull away, Buster's grip would tighten ever so slightly.

Over a period of time, we collected quite a menagerie, most of which had been abandoned or unwanted. Buster took responsibility for them all.

On one occasion, he stood at the field fence, whining and whinging, refusing to come when we called. When Tony went to investigate, he found that one of our cats was caught up in the Forestry's barbed wire by her fur and had become impossibly entangled. I had to take him some scissors to cut her free. On another occasion, Buster made the same agitated sound while standing near my strawberry bed. When we got there, we discovered that a skylark had become trapped under the strawberry netting and was frantically fluttering to get out. Tony lifted the netting, and the little bird flew straight up into the sky, singing her thanks all the way.

Tony had made a nursery for those hens which had produced chicks and surrounded them with a substantial pen of chicken wire. Buster lay beside the pen, making those whinging sounds that told us something was wrong. When we reached him, he had a huge paw on one of the day-old chicks that had managed to slip through the chicken wire and was unable to find its way back. His paws were about as big as a teacup, but he had managed to restrain the chick without hurting it until one of us put it back in the pen with its mother.

I think one of the most amazing things he did was to take a mouse from one of our cats. The cat was tormenting the mouse, letting it run and then jumping on it, and then repeating the torture, playing with it. Buster brought the mouse to me and laid it at my feet. By this time, the poor little creature was catatonic, rigid with fear, lying on its back with its legs in the air, not moving. I truly thought it was dead. So, Buster nudged it with his nose to make it twitch and prove to me that it was still alive. I told him to take it outside. He picked it up, the tail hanging out of the side of his mouth, and carried it outside. When I gave him the command to "leave it," he placed it gently on the ground. After a few moments, as we watched, he and I, the mouse sat up, cleaned Buster's saliva from its eyes and nose, and then it ran off through the grass.

He made it his job to keep the peace between the cockerels, and when they sparred, he would jump on them and chase off the bird that had started the fight. He also understood how to herd cattle if they strayed onto our land.

Buster would escort them out of the gate and along the track towards the road, and if one happened to wander into the bog, he would go around it and bring it back to the others. Joe, who owned the bullocks, told us that he was convinced that Buster would scatter them when they reached the road. Sure enough, at the end of our track, half the herd turned towards Joe and half turned away.

Buster ran beyond the few that had gone the wrong way and gently and calmly brought them back to Joe and the rest of the group. Nobody taught him; he simply figured it out for himself. Joe told us he had no concerns about Buster being around his cattle now.

Our dog was friendly with Anne and Frit's Alsatian bitch called Verity. When her owners were out for the day, Verity was not allowed to venture any further from their cottage than a small bridge that marked the limit of Frit's property. Crossing that bridge was forbidden. One day, lo and behold, we arrived home to find Verity at the junction of the track and the lane. Tony ordered her to "go home," but she stubbornly refused. Nor would she get into our car. Buster positioned his body alongside hers, shoulder to shoulder. They ran as though yoked together along the track ahead of our car, around the bend at the end of the valley, and as far as Frit's bridge. It was a total distance of about one-third of a mile. He escorted Verity across the bridge while we watched and then turned and came home, leaving her there. How did he know?

His understanding, sense of fair play, and ability to communicate were far beyond normal canine intelligence. I couldn't help but feel that there was an exceptionally kind and caring individual inside him, and that he possessed attributes that we, as humans, could well aspire to. Buster was truly remarkable.

We were soon given another dog to keep Buster and the two cats company.

He was the last survivor of a litter of nine. All the others had died one way or another (I didn't question it too deeply). Tina brought him home and asked us to toilet train him, and then she would have him back to live with her. Of course, he never went back. We settled him in a shoebox under the table with Tina's "Panda" slippers as his "mum" and named him Bobby.

Bobby grew into a big dog with an exceptionally thick coat to rival Narla's. He was a gentle soul, very calm and laid back. He was the carer and nursemaid for the other animals. When Wendy's Lurcher turned up at our house during a thunderstorm, terrified and wet through, shaking with fear and cold, it was Bobby who lay alongside her until she stopped shaking and helped her to dry off.

While Bobby was still a puppy, we acquired a third dog, a Jack Russell. Jack had twice jumped into Tina's car with a year between each event. On the first occasion, she dropped him off at the nearest houses in the hope that he would find his own way home. On the second occasion, he had a multitude of cuts on his face as though he had either been in a fight or been hit by a car. She brought him to us. Tony had to put on leather gauntlets to handle him, and he gently cleaned up the poor dog's face. It was Bobby who took over the job of keeping Jack's wounds clean, constantly licking his face. I tried to find Jack's owner without success, so he stayed.

But Jack was a killer, true to his breed. If any of our animals seemed to be in difficulties or ailing, Jack would attack them, whether it was a hen having a dust bath and fluttering, or if the young Bobby squealed in his sleep, which he sometimes did, or even, on one occasion, much to our amusement, the horse went down to have a roll and Jack jumped on his neck to finish him off.

The final dog of our "pack" was a mongrel pup that Tina nearly ran over late at night on the Coast Road in Oranmore. He was a very busy little dog and very vocal. He was the best guard dog of the four of them. As with Jack, I tried to find his owner. The keeper of the pound in Ennis told me that if no one claimed him after three days, then we could be certain that he had been abandoned. He also told me that he had just had to explain to a student helping him why he was about to put down forty-nine dogs that day. I was appalled. Of course, we kept the pup, named Scamp, but throughout his life, we couldn't get him to go into the car, leaving me thinking that perhaps he had been thrown out of a moving vehicle onto the Coast Road where Tina found him.

Chapter Eight

At about the same time that Bobby joined us, we took in a ten-month-old cat called Aravis. She lived at Kate and Neil's with her owner, but Neil was moving out, Kate and her children were going back to England, and Aravis' owner was moving to a flat which didn't welcome animals. Aravis was going to be euthanised so we took her home.

We learnt that they had abandoned some bantams in their barn, and there was also a little white cat that was surviving on what she could catch.

Tony took a bucket of feed to the bantams and ended up bringing them all home. Aravis brought the white cat home, and I caught her in a cat basket with some food. She was fairly wild but responded to food, warmth, and a little love. She was also pregnant and went into labour on my knee. I laid her in a box and sat with her while she produced four kittens. Aravis used to babysit, allowing the kittens to suckle on her, even though she had no milk, while Sweetie, the hunter, would go off to provide the fresh meat. It worked very well. Wendy had one of the kittens, another neighbour in the valley had another, and we kept two, Yoda and Corky. Aravis lived to twenty-three, but she never liked being picked up. She liked being stroked and petted, but only on the floor. Apparently, her previous owner would throw her out of a window if he found her indoors.

We eventually ended up with eight cats. One large ginger cat stayed with us for a couple of months. We called him Jaffa. Jaffa was a whole male, totally unapproachable. We fed him in one of the stables where we kept the chest freezer. I thought he was making a terrible mess in there, and I was determined that he should be neutered. We caught him and took him to the vet. When we brought him back and set him free, we never saw him again. I can't say I blame him. However, the mess in the stable continued, and I discovered that it wasn't Jaffa but a pine marten who was enjoying the cat food meant for Jaffa. Out came the mink trap, baited with smelly fish. The pine marten was taken several miles up the road towards Lough Atoric and set loose. He scampered off into the forestry.

The final cat in our collection was a little calico cat called Gypsy. She and her siblings were left in a box at a junction a few hundred yards up the lane. We found homes for the others and kept Gypsy. She spent most of her time in the polytunnel or in the stable. She never made any mess in the house, and I didn't have to house-train her. She would come in for a cuddle in the evening and then disappear until morning.

We had been in Ireland for two years when Stuart and Wendy finally managed to get here. They had to wait for the housing market in the UK to improve before they could sell their property in Helston. They brought their animals with them, and since we now had fencing around our fields, their two ponies joined Basil, and their Lurcher, cats, and some poultry were billeted in a small caravan, which we had bartered for a roll of chicken wire. Stu took on the job of breakfast chef, and then they were off house hunting until the evening meal. Sleeping accommodation was no problem as they slept in their own panel van. After six weeks or so, they happily settled for some land about a mile and a half from where we were living. For several years, we helped and encouraged each other with our building projects, and Tony and Wendy stepped in to look after the other's animals if the owner was on holiday or needed in England.

Once Wendy's animals were comfortably housed on her own land, Kate let Tony "borrow" a grey mare, a three-quarter Thoroughbred called Smokey, for Tina to ride, and she included a pregnant pony called April for him to care for as well. April was a clever little pony and a proper Houdini. (She once watched me arrange some branches to close up a break in the hedge, and when I had finished, she took it apart in the exact reverse order in which I had laid them.) Each night, we would walk the horses back to Kate's farm for stabling. A few weeks later, I noticed that Basil kept pushing April away. He wouldn't let her anywhere near himself nor Smokey. Finally, fed up with what appeared to be bullying, she escaped and trotted back to Kate's farm. She produced a beautiful little foal that night. April and the foal were returned to whoever owned them in the first place. But Smokey stayed with us for what Kate called "permanent loan." Our menagerie was growing.

While we were collecting our pack of dogs, we also acquired other stock. In the spring of 1996, we took in Snowdrop, the Saanen goat, and Narla, the Texel cross sheep. We hoped that Snowdrop would eventually provide us with milk, and I had high hopes of learning how to turn Narla's fleece into Aran sweaters.

It was Tina who noticed that Snowdrop was producing the precursor of milk and began to encourage the flow. I must admit to being relieved that Snowdrop was a maiden milker because I hadn't come to terms with the prospect of disposing of any unwanted offspring to guarantee a regular supply of milk. Bless her; she gave us eight pints a day during the spring and summer and two pints a day during the autumn and winter. And that was all her life for eleven years without the need to introduce her to a billy goat. But she and I had a love/hate relationship. Tina could milk her. Tony could milk her. But she wouldn't give me a drop. The only explanation I can think of is that she considered Tina and Tony her "babies" and saw me as a threat. Or perhaps I gave out the wrong vibes.

Snowdrop was sometimes a liability. She would eat anything and everything, from the fruit trees to the washing on the laundry line. I planted out twenty-five strawberry runners for Wendy to collect, and I left them overnight on top of a low wall. The following day, the plants were strewn all over the garden along with twenty-five empty pots. Mind you, the culprit may have been the deer. The jury is still out.

But we certainly had plenty of goat's milk. I made "Poor Man's Cheese" using cheesecloth, and I experimented with making yogurt overnight in a vacuum flask. It worked quite well. There was even enough to give to a neighbour who suffered from psoriasis, like Tony. Tony would drink it or have it on his cereal on the first day, but the milk seemed to acquire a stronger taste after that. Tina and I could not bring ourselves to drink it at all.

Basil and Snowdrop were the best of buddies. Theirs was a symbiotic relationship. In wet weather, Snowdrop would stand underneath Basil's chest for shelter, and Basil would scratch his chin contentedly on her horns. We tied an old tyre to her collar in an attempt to limit her escapes and slow her down, but she worked out that if she managed to get the tyre onto its tread, it would roll, and she happily gambolled about the fields with the tyre rolling along behind her.

Narla and Snowdrop each had a pen in the third stable where the hay and straw were stored. They tolerated each other well except when Narla was sheared. Perhaps she smelled differently, or looked strange, but it was as if Snowdrop didn't recognise her. She would chase her and knock seven bells out of the poor sheep until her fleece grew again.

We had to take Narla to the vet because she developed a swollen ear flap. Between us pushing and a bucket of feed, we managed to get her into the back of the estate. At the vet's, we were directed around the back of the building to an open concreted area, and Tony persuaded Narla to jump out of the car. She was a big, heavy, overweight animal. The vet gave her a sedative, assuring us that it wouldn't put her to sleep but was just to keep her calm and pain-free. Narla was as good as gold, standing behind the car while the vet operated on her ear, drained it, and stitched it up. As he walked away, job done, Narla collapsed on the ground, sound asleep. It took all three of us to manhandle her back into the car. On the way home, she roused herself and stood up with her mouth right behind Tony's ear. She let out a belch, and, believe me, there is nothing worse than the smell of regurgitated silage. We had paused at some traffic lights with the windows down and heard a little girl say to her mother, "Mummy, look at that big doggie in the back of that car!" I wonder what "Mummy" thought of it.

Basil and Smokey needed exercising, so we erected some jumps in the top field. Tina had been riding since she was six, and she and her dad would take part in their inter-club competitions in Cornwall. Basil loved to jump, but Smokey had never been introduced to it, so Tina decided to try and teach her. Unlike Basil, she was not a natural jumper. With Tina on board, they approached the jump at a fair canter. Smokey refused and applied the brakes, stopping dead in front of the bar, with the result that Tina sailed horizontally between the horse's ears. As she flew through the air and then slid along the ground, she was heard yelling "WICKED!" at the top of her voice, much to the amusement of the people who had gathered to watch.

When Kate and Niall left the area, their farm was empty for about a month.

We heard that they had left some bantams behind in the barn, so Tony took a bucket of feed to them. They would have followed that bucket all the way back to our property, so we brought them home. Ducks came next. At first, simply because they were pretty, we had a pair of Apple yards that looked very much like Mallards. Khaki Campbells came next for their eggs, then the big, white Aylesbury ducks, supposedly for the table. Of course, they never reached the table. We ended up with eleven ducks, a dozen laying hens, and thirty-six bantams of all different colours.

We had quite a menagerie.

Chapter Nine

Narla was about seven when we noticed a growth in her nose. We described it to the vet over the phone. He told me very brusquely that it could be any one of three things, all of which were fatal. I said, "Hang on a minute. This is a pet." His manner changed. "Alright," he said. "Bring her down." But the prognosis didn't change. Either the growth would grow outwards and interfere with her breathing or else back towards her brain. As long as she was not in any discomfort, we decided to leave her alone. A few months later, while Tony was in England, she died in her sleep.

Smokey, Tina's grey mare, wasn't with us very long either. Tina and her father would go out for rides together, which both they and the horses enjoyed, but there are no bridal paths in our area such as they were used to in Cornwall; here are forestry tracks, but those are out of bounds for insurance reasons, and most have a locked barrier across to stop both traffic and livestock. Roadwork meant frequent shoeing. Basil was quite used to that and would stand happily on three legs for the farrier. Tony always had him hot-shod in England, which were a better fit, but the travelling farrier had no electric "forge," and Basil was always losing his shoes, sucked off in the mud.

Smokey would wait patiently for her turn with the farrier. Then, suddenly, there would be an almighty thump. It was Smokey falling down. Horses can sleep on their feet, but they have to lock their knees. Smokey would forget to lock her forelegs, she would drift off to sleep, and collapse. It happened once while the farrier was shoeing her. The poor man thought he had killed her.

Although Basil was a gelding, he considered Smokey his mare, and it was a great sight to watch them, freed of their saddles and bridles, just run unencumbered across the hill. Tony had borrowed the adjacent field from Annie, and at the end of the day, he would call both horses, and they would race back at a full gallop, through the gate, up the drive, and into their own stable for their evening feed.

During the good weather, they were fed outside in the field, and Basil's dominance was apparent. He had to be fed first, and then Smokey, otherwise, he would put her off the feed bowl. After they had eaten, Tony would send Buster in to collect the feed bowls. If Basil was still being possessive about an empty feed bowl, Buster would bark at him, get the horse to chase him, and then the dog would circle back and pick up the bowl. It was a great game.

When she was twelve, Smokey fell ill, and the vet had to be called. He diagnosed summer mastitis. Her condition continued to deteriorate, and she was obviously in considerable discomfort. We could see by the path she had trodden in the stable that she had been walking round and round. Tony stayed up all the next night with her, but it was clear that there was something seriously wrong. She was literally dying on her feet. I called the vet to euthanise the poor animal but she died in Tony's arms in her stable. The vet eventually came and revised his opinion. He thought it likely that her liver had been damaged by eating ragwort as a young filly. Apparently, ragwort is poisonous to horses, and even more so if it is dried. It could have been in the hay she had eaten, and her owner would have known nothing about it.

This particular paragraph is hard to write and not for the faint-hearted.

Smokey died in her stable on a Monday, 13th November. We could not have her taken away until Wednesday, 15th, which just happened to be Tony's birthday. The lorry was too heavy to get along the bog road to the stable, so we asked Joe if he would bring his big tractor to drag Smokey out of the stable, down the driveway, and along the quarter-mile stretch of gravelled access road as far as the lane where the lorry was parked. Because of the two-day delay, her carcass had bloated, the smell was gut-wrenching, and by the time our sad cortege reached the knacker's lorry, her body had split, and her entrails were dragging along behind her. There was a bloody track a yard wide all along the access road. When we reached the lane, a chain was attached to one of Smokey's hind legs, and this noble, beloved animal was unceremoniously hoisted into the lorry and dropped onto all the other cadavers.

Tony and I decided that, from that day on, none of our animals would ever leave the property again.

Chapter Ten

Of course, as well as the animals we accumulated, there was also a richness of wild fauna, some of which was most unwelcome. From the beginning of April until October, we were tormented by midges. The female of these tiny flies is a heat-seeking missile. They would appear as the sun came up, and they would be a metre deep around the caravan. They would disappear if the day was hot and then reappear in the early evening, attracted by the gas lamps above the table in the van. They flew up to the lamp, kamikaze-style, burned, died, and dropped to the table beneath. By the end of the evening, there was a pile big enough to make a sandwich filling!

I felt so sorry for the animals. The midges would go for the moisture in the eyes, and sometimes the faces of the horses and the goat would be black with them. We would wipe the animals' faces with a cloth soaked in anti-midge solution, but nothing worked satisfactorily. At night, we could hear the poor horses constantly on the move in an effort to escape the horrible little insects. We tried to work through them by covering our heads and faces with netting and smothering ourselves with a deterrent, but the only real solution was to drive away as far as the Burren. The midges don't seem to tolerate limestone. Happily, once the house was built, the problem eased somewhat, presumably because of the lime in the concrete.

We had two pairs of pheasants that visited us frequently. Of course, we put down corn for them. They brought their clutch of chicks for us to enjoy, making us feel very honoured. The corn attracted the deer, both the Roe deer and the little Sika deer. They would graze in our fields quite happily alongside the horses and the goat. Strangely, the cats never bothered the pheasants or their chicks. If we met a deer while taking the dogs for a walk, Buster would immediately give chase, but if they were grazing on our land, he guarded them as diligently as he did our domesticated animals. It was as though he had decided that if they were on our land, then they belonged and it was his responsibility to keep them safe. We had a magnificent black stag resting under a tree in our lower field. He had antlers with a spread of four feet. After four days, we didn't see him again, and we prayed that he hadn't been shot by the trophy hunters. The following spring we were pleased to see several unusually dark youngsters appear with their proud mums.

We liked to see the fox but not near the chickens. Mr Fox came in broad daylight and took our two ornamental ducks off the pond. All Buster found was a wing, which he brought back to me. We tried very hard to keep the chickens and the ducks safe from the fox, and we were quite successful. A fox will only take what he (or she) needs, especially if she has cubs. Usually, they will take their catch away, unlike the pine marten and the mink.

The pine marten killed several of our chickens by apparently climbing through the roof of the chicken coop. He came back the next night and killed the ducks, leaving the bodies in a neat line. But the mink was the worst. He took all thirty-six bantams in one night. The Jack Russell tried to drive him off, but the mink retaliated, and Jack was quite badly bitten. He must have done damage to the mink as well because the creature didn't come back. We trapped the pine marten and took him several miles up the road away from farms and houses and released him.

We fed the smaller birds as well as the pheasants. There must have been a dozen swallows' nests around the house and the stables every year. They would be in each of the stables, and parent birds would fly in between the horses' ears through the stable doors. More nests would appear in the top of the gable ends, under the eaves, and beside the front and back doors. They loved the stonework for attaching their nests, and while the house was being built, they would fly in and out of the empty windows. Unfortunately, once the glass was in, the poor little birds would crash against the new glass and drop to the ground. Then it was a race to see if we could save the injured bird before a cat picked it up. Usually, after an hour or so in a quiet room in a box, the bird was ready to depart.

Tony and I used to have breakfast every Sunday in a cafe in Ballina, across the bridge from Killaloe. There are two enormous trees just on the Ballina side which are very popular with a colony of rooks. As we were passing, we saw a chick which had probably fallen out of a nest, all beak and feet. It had already fallen about fifty feet through the branches of the tree and was vulnerable to dogs and pedestrians walking past. Tony moved it to the protection of some roots and said that if it was still there when we returned, we would take it home.

And, of course, it was still there where Tony had placed it.

We acquired a cardboard box from a nearby shop and took the chick home. Tony made a nest for it, and I hand-fed it with mashed up cat food every hour. We didn't expect it to survive after such a bad start, but it thrived. He was called Buddy. Buddy outgrew his nest, and Tony moved him to a large cage outside. Eventually, it was obvious that buddy wanted to try out his wings. His maiden flight was a disaster. He crashed into the wall of an outbuilding and fluttered away into a ditch. Tony waded in and rescued him. Buddy gradually got the idea, and he would return to the cage when Tony called him, and he would land on Tony's arm to be offered titbits. His favourite was chocolate digestives.

We began to notice that Buddy wasn't eating what we gave him, but he was hiding it in holes in the ground or cracks in the walls or fencing, cleverly covering it up with pieces of moss. (The dogs would watch where Buddy buried his food and would help themselves to his stash once he had flown away.) It was obvious that Buddy was eating elsewhere. It was time for him to go. For several days, he would overfly the property without landing, and then he disappeared.

We missed him. I'd like to think that he joined a rookery and produced his own family.

One year, Tony and I witnessed a marvellous phenomenon. It was the last day of September, the 30th. We became aware of a strange sound, like a loud rushing wind or like white water rapids. We looked out of the window and were amazed. There were billions, literally billions, of swallows flying in a continuous ellipse over the bog below us in the valley. They were flying the length of the valley, about a quarter of a mile, just above the vegetation, then curving back towards the road at a height of about thirty feet. This aerial ballet continued for several hours, and the noise of their beating wings and their twittering was deafening. The next morning, all the swallows in the area had gone. There was silence. It must have been a feeding frenzy with the insects on the bog, the bog myrtle, and the sedge grass, before the birds had to make their three-thousand-mile journey to South Africa. Or perhaps they just came to say "Goodbye." The summer was over.

Chapter Eleven

We Begin the Building

After Christmas was over that first year, we turned our attention to the problem of providing ourselves with permanent accommodation. We reopened the precious book that I had brought back from my trip to America and reread the instructions for making the wooden forms which we would be bolting together top and bottom and to each other horizontally. Two forms would be placed opposite each other and held apart by wiring them together against a wooden spacer, the length of which would determine the thickness of the wall.

Tony was the designated carpenter.

We soon encountered a couple of problems. Firstly, Tony's eyes were developing cataracts, and although a line for sawing is, theoretically, not supposed to have any thickness, we had to use a highlighting pen for Tony to see it. The second problem was that he was stuck in the pre-decimal era and would only use feet and inches. Of course, any building materials, as well as the instructions on the plans, were in metric. So, we compromised. We made four-foot, six-foot, and eight-foot forms, and I transposed the measurements on the plans to feet and inches. We tried bolting straight forms together at ninety degrees to create the corners, but soon found that they were not satisfactory. So, Tony made two sets of corners for the internal and external bend, with a length of four foot in either direction. They were very heavy, but they worked far better.

We needed a trial run with the forms, so we thought of making a walled garden eight feet square and with walls nine inches thick. The surface of our forms was marine ply, and we liberally painted them with used engine oil begged from the local garage so that they would come away from the cement more easily. We dug some shallow foundations, mixed up the concrete in a wheelbarrow with my trusty ditching spade, and poured the footings. After it dried, we set up the forms so as to include two adjacent corner units in the belief that they would be self-bracing, wired them together with fencing wire through previously drilled holes at two-foot intervals, and tightened the wire by twisting it with a used nail against a nine-inch spacer. The wire and the nail would remain in the wall, and anything showing on the outside could be trimmed off when the stones were grouted with mortar. Lastly, and very importantly, I used a builder's level and diligently checked that the forms were both vertical and horizontal. If they were slightly out of true, we would buttress them with wooden stakes. It sounds like a lot of faffing about, but we soon got the hang of it.

It became an obsession with me to collect stones that had at least one flat face. Oh, the excitement when we found a whole nest of suitable stones lurking in a ditch or under a hedge. It was an unwritten rule that we wouldn't help ourselves to any stone that was performing a useful purpose, so the local walls remained intact and farm gates wedged open with a lump of limestone; however perfectly formed, the gate remained wedged. I set myself a target of collecting twenty stones a day. I walked in the forestry and scoured the side of the tracks. I negotiated with the farmers to allow me to walk their fields. I asked for permission to search ruined outbuildings for likely candidates, especially large corner stones. They were diamonds. When you think about it, I needed to collect at least four hundred tons of stone, a house-sized pile. I even had a large piece of Cornish granite and a couple of pieces of Norfolk flint built into the walls.

I chose my stones carefully for the little walled garden so that they would more or less fit together and would look attractive with a mixture of sandstone and limestone. Also, of course, they had to overlap each other for strength.

Tony and I took turns to mix the concrete in the wheelbarrow and carried it in a bucket to the building site. The concrete was pressed firmly at the bottom of the forms, and a suitable stone was bedded in the concrete with the flat face to the outside, then another was pressed in beside it, leaving a small gap between. Repeating the process, we gradually filled the forms to the top. After two days allowing the concrete to dry, we were able to unveil this work of art and move on. If the weather was wet or threatened frost, we would cover the work with sacking. We soon learnt that the marine ply wasn't suitable. It tended to warp with the moisture in the cement and made it difficult to level the forms and make them vertical. So, Tony rebuilt them using larch for the surfaces, which we kept oiled. They lasted for years. We soon had a small, walled flower garden. The system worked. It was laborious and time-consuming, but it worked. Time to get planning permission.

Niall, who had helped position the caravan originally, was also an architect, and his partner, Kate, bullied him into providing us with plans "pro bono." We duly submitted them, but they were refused. The lady from Bord Planola, who had come to inspect the site, had been met by three of our dogs and another two belonging to Wendy and Stuart. She had turned up in open-toed sandals and beige slacks. Considering that this was a building site and pretty muddy as well, I thought with hindsight that she was improperly dressed for the task. It was not a very fortuitous beginning. The reason given for refusing the planning permission was that the access road was unsuitable for heavy traffic in the case of an emergency such as an ambulance or a fire engine. But I can't help thinking that the dogs had something to do with it.

Anyway, I wrote a careful letter to her at Bord Planola, telling her that we were not satisfied with the access road either and had already commissioned a local man to clear out the ditch alongside the track and put down more gravel on the top of the existing surface. I resubmitted the planning request, and this time it passed.

The problem with the track was that it had been laid down on top of a blanket bog and was only intended for walkers, or perhaps a donkey cart in days gone by. Any traffic heavier than eight tons would have cracked the surface and got stuck. So all our building materials had to be unloaded at the road end and then ferried up to our property with the car. We needed something more robust, like a tractor and trailer.

But, first things first. We needed a bridge to get across the stream that ran alongside the track at the bottom of our fields. So, we had five concrete rings delivered, each three feet long and two feet in diameter, and with Frit's help and his little tractor, we lowered them into the stream. Frit cleverly butted them securely together, standing in the water, and we had the makings of a bridge. The next step was to surround the rings with rubble and cover the whole thing with concrete between forms. Several wheelbarrow loads of concrete later and we had our bridge.

Frit was allowed to etch the words "FRIT WOS 'ERE" in the surface for posterity. That is still there.

We eventually completed a stone and gravel driveway from the bridge to the caravan, a distance of about a hundred metres. We also acquired a tractor and trailer. And I had the honour of christening the completed driveway by driving the tractor up the slope and parking it near our home.

Chapter Twelve

One cold, windy, drizzly morning in December 1998, I looked across the fields from the caravan window, and the two horses were standing in a corner, hunched and miserable. We had to provide them with some form of shelter while we built the house. Tony suggested that we erect a field shelter. We acquired ten discarded telephone poles and sank them in the ground at the bottom end of the field in a C-shape with the intention of surrounding them with palette wood. Somehow, that never materialised, and Tony's "ten pillars of wisdom," as we called them, were eventually dismantled and sawn up for firewood.

Our priority was obviously to build the stables.

Tony wanted three stables and a tack room, so we decided on nine-inch stone exterior walls with block dividing partitions. Tony would build the interior walls, tying them into my stonework. There would be oak lintels over each door, and Tony would make split doors for the three stables and a full door for the tack/feed room. Basil and Smokey would each have a stable, and the third stable would store the bales of hay and straw.

So, we took turns to dig out the footings. And, being winter, the trench we dug was constantly filling with water which we had to drain with a pipe running down the infant driveway. We thought later that we might have ruptured an ancient land drain. The answer was to dig out a sump hole in one corner to drain off the excess water. As the days got longer and the weather warmer, we mixed load after load of cement in the trusty wheelbarrow, first for the footings, then, as I began raising the exterior walls, the floor was laid with the damp-proof course, and then the interior block walls. Tony had completed four rows of the first wall when we had a night of very high winds, rattling the caravan. The following morning the whole block wall was on the floor.

We put another damp-proof course in the walls about two feet from the floor in case of moisture from the bedding working its way upwards. Then we laid a second concrete floor on top of the first one in each stable. I remember that there were thirty-six of my wheelbarrow loads to each stable floor. And it wasn't until we were working on the final stable that we could afford to buy a cement mixer. We also purchased a little Massey Ferguson tractor (Tony's pride and joy) and a trailer, which made the task of transporting the sand, the gravel, and timbers from the end of the track much easier. That tractor was the first vehicle to travel up our driveway.

Once the horses were comfortable, we could finally turn our attention to the building of the house.

After talking it over, we decided that we would build the three bedrooms and the bathroom first and use one of the bedrooms as a living room while we built the other half of the house. (Our son joked that he wouldn't visit us until we had a proper flush toilet.) We had to have a water supply, electricity, and some form of sewerage.

The house was to have walls two feet thick with insulation in the middle, so we started digging out the footings, four feet wide and 2 feet 6 inches deep. Of course, there was the familiar sound of a spade on stone, and we came to recognise whether it was just a stone or a rock or mountain just from the sound. Some rocks we prized out with the spade, some we had to lever out using stakes to prop them up while we placed smaller rocks underneath, and repeated the process until the offending stone was at ground level. One major stone obstacle was hauled out using the car, and still another was simply left in the trench because it was part of the mountain. Every stone was put to use somewhere else, either on the driveway or as a possible building stone.

It took us three months to dig out the footings for the first half of the house, from May through July. With load after load of concrete, we filled the huge trench and had to step the concrete to accommodate a slight slope in the ground. If we could have brought machinery up the track to level the site before we built on it, and if we could have had a digger to excavate the trench for us, a cement lorry to deliver and pour the concrete footings, then, how much easier it would have been!

We wrestled with the forms to get them accurately placed and bolted together, and filled them to the level of the damp-proof course. We filled the centre with hardcore and tamped it down with a hired whacker plate. Four inches of concrete went in next, followed by 50mm insulation, and a gas-proof membrane over both the floor and the walls, then another four inches of concrete. It was now November. Unfortunately, a couple of nights after we had finished the floor, we had a hard frost, and the top layer crumbled to dust. We asked a local builder whether we could get a cement leveller that would flow over the concrete, but he told us that, now, we would never get a decent floor.

We would have to have a "floating floor" of tongue and groove attached to wooden struts. So, we settled for that.

As we worked away at the walls, we contacted an electrician about getting electricity to the site. Because we had stables, we could get a certificate for providing power to an agricultural building, and then we could add whatever we wanted for the house. The metre box had to be incorporated in a gable end, and a waterproof membrane had to be built in to prevent any rain seeping into the box. A man plus mini-digger made the trench to take the cable across our land, and I was fascinated watching him work. He danced that bucket or hook around as though he were choreographing a ballet. He took down a fence and the stakes with his hook, and replaced them afterwards without getting out of his cab. I laughingly asked him to save any stones with a flat face, and, bless him, he did, lifting them up with his hook and lining them up along the side of the trench!

Our electrician came back, and we had lights in each stable and the tack room, double outlets for attaching an electric fence or a chest freezer or tools if the need arose, and decorative lights on the stables. It made feeding the horses in the winter months much easier.

The electrician also gave us a temporary feed to the caravan. For several years, our daughter had been forced to do her homework by candlelight and gas light. Now, she bought us a small television, and my husband could have the choice of watching his favourite programs or retiring to the bedroom to listen to his audio-tapes. What a luxury electricity was!

Tony had to make several trips to England while the building continued. His mother was widowed and elderly, and her health was deteriorating. He would be away for varying lengths of time, the longest being four months. (The village grapevine was convinced that he had left me.) I became the sole builder while he was away. But I must add that the neighbours kept an eye on me. Our friend, Wendy, dropped by on her bicycle every day to make sure that I was not lying at the bottom of a ladder.

I carefully incorporated eight-inch bolts in the top level on either side, ensuring they were perfectly vertical. These bolts would secure the roof plates firmly in place. We then applied a good dollop of white paint to the top end of each bolt and positioned the wooden beam, allowing the paint to mark where each bolt protruded from the concrete. Tony could then drill a hole in the beam for each bolt. We offered the beam up again, and, lo and behold, each bolt slid neatly through each hole, and we were able to tighten down the nuts to hold the roof plate in place. I could then work away at the two gable ends, allowing for where the rafters would disappear into the stonework. Since we had no builder's instructions with the building plans, I had to try and think ahead. For instance, I incorporated a thick length of wood to follow the line of the roof to the entrance hall to insert the lead flashing, although the hall wasn't yet built. When the extension was finally constructed, that piece of wood could come out. And I had to allow for the walls of the second half of the building to be tied into the completed half.

We employed an English neighbour to do the roofing of this first half, and the windows and doors were commissioned in teak to the measurements I gave and double glazed. We "foamed" them in with the help of Stuart and Wendy, who had experience fixing window frames in their stone cottage in Cornwall; then, we cemented over the join to make them weatherproof.

Tony started on the interior studwork, and the rooms began to take shape.

The flooring throughout the house was tongue and groove, and the interior walls had four inches of insulation. Now we needed a plumber. We had decided that we would harvest the rainwater from the roof, so we had a large tank sunk in the ground so that it would never freeze, and Tony built a pump house beside it. The rain flowed into the guttering, through the downpipe, and passed through a pipe underground into the huge tank. It was then pumped back up to the holding tank in the roof space. In the twenty years or so before we had the well dug, that tank only dried up once, the pump froze and cracked twice, and we chose to filter our drinking water, but it worked. Now we could create a bathroom and get the electricity installed.

I still had no proper kitchen, and I was still cooking in the caravan. So, we created a makeshift kitchen in the reception hallway. Tony had closed off the doorway leading into the other half of the house (which we had yet to build), and we installed the gas cooker in the potential doorway. A table served as a countertop, and we carried water in for washing dishes and food preparation.

We also had to consider a sewage system. Because of the lack of topsoil, we knew that a percolation system would not pass. A reed bed was not practical.

The only answer was a bio-system. The blurb advertised that, after being treated in two tanks, one aerobic and the other anaerobic, the outflow of the effluent that ended up in the stream could actually be drunk! I wouldn't like to try it! But we went ahead and had the system installed. I have it maintained every January, and it is still working well.

When it came to measuring out the second half of the house, the half that had the chimney, we came upon a big problem. The caravan was in the way. A corner of the house would be sticking through the side of the van. It wasn't possible to continue.

Tony worked away at the obstructing part of the caravan wall with an angle grinder until there was room for me to stand. We wrestled the forms in place, meticulously measuring from corner to corner to ensure we had an accurate rectangle. Even a centimetre out at this level could mean several centimetres out by the time we had reached roof level. We also had to mark out the position of the chimney. The chimney breast was to be quite massive to accommodate a stove with a back boiler, and the foundation for it was to be six feet by four feet and a metre deep. That's a lot of concrete. I didn't feel confident enough to build the chimney, so I persuaded a neighbour to build it in block, and another neighbour was willing to put in the hearth of Liscannor stone and to face the block to match the walls. A large piece of timber served as a mantel.

We had to borrow the money from the bank to complete the tiling of the roof. We had enough money to pay for the windows and exterior doors but could not afford both the roof and the windows. We took out a loan and agreed to pay it back over a five-year period.

The rendering of the interior walls of the second half of the house was a disaster. I had picked out the plasterer from a newspaper advert. The good rule book says that you start with the ceiling and then do the walls, but these lads proceeded with the walls and then tried to do the ceilings, with the result that there was a gap all around the room where the wall and ceiling met. It teemed all day, which made it very difficult for them to mix the render to the right consistency. After the walls were thoroughly dry, Tony had to patch the render in places and fill the gap where the walls met the ceilings. He tried to make a neat finish, but all we could do in the end was to fix polystyrene moulding around the room to cover the shoddy workmanship.

Tony spent his seventieth birthday laying the tongue and groove floor in the second half of the house with help from friends and family who had gathered to celebrate the occasion. I had originally tiled the entrance hall while it served as a kitchen, but we decided to continue the wood floor all the way through.

Over the next two years, we had plenty of plumbing work done. Radiators were installed in the bedrooms and the bathroom, which was now fitted with a proper suite and an "over-bath" shower, and a stove with a back boiler was installed on the stone hearth in the open-plan living room for the radiators and domestic hot water. Finally, my grandson Christopher, over in England, had negotiated to save an entire kitchen that was going to be thrown away. It was in perfect condition, complete with a Miele dishwasher. He came over to Ireland with his father to install my new kitchen, and all we had to buy was the countertops. And with an unoccupied stable, we could have a washing machine and a spin drier. Eventually, we had a fridge in the kitchen and a large chest freezer in the stable.

It had taken twelve years from start to finish.

Epilogue

We lived at "Moonfleet" for twenty-five years, as close to self-sufficiency as was practical. We had good friends and neighbours, although we watched out for each other without living in each other's pockets. There was always someone with a tractor to pull a car out of a ditch or to round up a horse off the road with a bucket of feed and a leading rope, or to help with a young cow having difficulties birthing a bull calf, or to provide a winch to get a horse onto his feet that had got himself cast.

There was always a welcome when we visited each other. The teapot would go on, and the soda bread would appear with butter and homemade jam. I am grateful for the evenings spent with Ann watching a video when we had no electricity, and the board games played with Wendy and Stuart. I shall never forget the neighbour who brought us a sack of logs and had to struggle through two feet of snow to bring it to us. And the two sisters, Bridie and Margaret, who always gave us a cup of tea on the way back from Gort. And, of course, the village shop at Flagmount where Annette and John kept us supplied and trusted that we would pay.

It was a very different place then. Now, the English "New Age Travellers," so-called, have moved on or bought land and settled. The drug culture certainly isn't so blatant, and we no longer have to listen to rave music until four in the morning. It seems that either we have returned to the rural Ireland of long ago, or respectability has moved in. I like to think that the good traditions of hospitality and tolerance have survived in our rural community.

As the years went on, we gradually lost our animals, although many of them lived to a good age. We decided not to replace them. Tony's health was deteriorating, and it was clear that we would have to retire to a town. We put the house on the market, but there was very little interest. So, we had a well dug to ensure that the water supply would never run dry and rented it out. It seemed that the era of self-sufficiency and choosing to live off the grid has passed, and the fields on which our horses, Basil and Smokey, Snowdrop the goat, and Narla the sheep grazed so contentedly have now gone back to nature.

We moved to Killaloe, Co. Clare, in 2019, just before the pandemic, and made it our home. We have a beautiful view of the mighty Shannon and of the sister town of Ballina across the river, but I must admit that there are times when I miss the space and the freedom of living on the side of our valley and the wonder of finding a Sika doe and her fawn on our front lawn.